ROUGH SEAS

To Shona
with best wishes
Tom Chew

The river is within us, the sea is all about us.
> T. S. Eliot, *Dry Salvages*

I want to know what it says . . . The sea, Floy, what it is that it keeps on saying.
> Charles Dickens, *Dombey and Son*

ROUGH SEAS
TOM POW

with wood engravings by Jonathan Gibbs

CANONGATE

First published in 1987
by Canongate Publishing Limited
17 Jeffrey Street, Edinburgh, Scotland

© 1987 Tom Pow
© wood engravings 1987 Jonathan Gibbs

British Library Cataloguing in Publication Data
Pow, Tom
Rough Seas.
I. Title
821'.914   PR6066.O8/
ISBN 0-86241-150-5

The publishers acknowledge the financial assistance
of the Scottish Arts Council
in the publication of this volume.

Some of these poems have appeared in
The Scotsman, Lines Review, Chapman, An Edinburgh Portrait
and *Le Hangar Ephemere*.

Typeset by Buccleuch Printers, Hawick, Scotland.
Printed and bound in Great Britain by Billings and Sons Limited,
Worcester.

for my mother and father

Contents

Invitation 7

I
Early Years 11
Half Day 12
The Judgement 14
Holiday down South 15
Mucking out the Byre 16
The King and Queen 18
The Master of Vailima 20
Words 22

II
The River 25
Film School 28
Declaration 29
Case Studies 30
Witches 31
Breakfast-Time 34
The Ship 36
A Favourite Stretch of Disused Railway 39
The Great Outdoors 42
Summer Running 43

III
Rough Seas: Three Postcards 47
Sisters 49
The Leap 52
Study in Iconography 54
The Rondanini Pietà 56
Catterline 58
Longing 59

Contents

IV

Absent Lover 63
In Central Park 64
Going Downtown 66
A Taxi of My Choice 68
The Bathers 70
Love at the (Bronx) Zoo 72
The Cabin 74
The Storm 76
Need 79
The Feast 80
Barges 82
Cagney Cuckolded in "The Roaring Twenties" 83
American Primitive 84
Natural History 86
Gospel 89
The Years 91
Still Life 92

Invitation

*Step through
the ragged hawthorn
into the park:
by a frozen pond
a muffled toddler
has absconded.
See her make
a clockwork run
at a scattering fan
of silver birds—
her open arms raised
in a gesture
of hopeless desire.*

I

Early Years

Each New Year, over a glass of sweet sherry,
she told the story of how they met.
She was sixteen and had travelled from Wick
with a friend. In a flurry
of snow he picked her up from the remote
station and took her to the farm
where she was taught
to cook flapjacks, befriend Indians, shoot
straight at grizzlies and stifle the blushes brought
on by the free curses of the ranchhand
who sat in her basin of dough.

Mostly though, they'd lived in Edinburgh
where George grew roses and worked for the GPO.
But they kept the bloom of those early years
well-watered: their two daughters lived them through
till their own ghostly youth was shelved.
Then alone, each night she kissed his photograph
and at New Year, giggled as she told
how that man had exploded: "Dough!
Thank God. I thought I'd ruptured myself."

Half Day

I

We lay in a hammock of grass and heather
below the broken neck of Arthur Seat:
the city around us like a lake of quartz,
yet here so still, so far from the buses
trawling Princes Street, we could hear crickets
clicking in the grass. We netted them
like minnows, from gently bowing stems;
coffined their green, quivering bodies
in a matchbox. Mother—impossibly young—
turned her face to the sun and we basked
in her ease and indifference: uniforms
rucked beneath us; nodules of heather gathered
on woollen socks. "Look, children, over there."
Her voice drifted down to us, airy as lace.
Even we hadn't noticed till it was
centre-stage: a childlike cumulus
over the ruined ark on Calton Hill.
Our eyes blinked in the brightness, the strangeness
of moving from our miniaturised world,
where heather stems were gnarled trees and crickets
roaring dragons, to this huge conjuring trick.
We had grown with the frail calligraphy
of aeroplanes, the rocket's scarlet bloom;
but there was magic in how this stayed afloat
and in a world which wanted it. More so
when mother told how they'd even made war
convivial—whole streets out to watch
as two droned over the shuttered city,
harmlessly released their bombs and chuntered off.
And this too looked so plumply good-natured,
you could never imagine it doing wrong,

allied as it was to the beneficent world
of circuses, balloons and giant combs.
We cast our darker selves in the heather
and stood up in the dizzying sun. If only
the power of our thoughts could hold it there,
or else a generous white fin scoop us home
(via the green Lothians, the shimmering Forth),
we would be saved from the workaday world
with its huffy queues and stuffy buses,
and mother's mouth stiffening in tiredness
on the final hill; the afternoon frittered . . .

II

All the dandelion clocks in the waste ground
had been blown to blind button-eyes, when we flicked
away spent grasshoppers, tight as beechbuds,
and joined the others in play. Our summer energy
was white-hot—we turned afternoon into
yesterday, easy as an old coat—
but the litmus of memory burned slower,
and that night, something passed over me in sleep;
high up, like the Leviathan that spreads
its ancient grey rafters over the City
Museum's cold gothic spaces; its flesh
hanging from it in tattered banners.

The Judgement

Such a small growl
my aunt's dachsund gave
as we both lay by the fire

then with a violent twist and a stab
she was gone.

Numb with shock, the blood
running down my cheek
was like tears.

When I looked up
my aunt had the bitch tucked neatly
between her feet.

"He must have been . . ."
"*Pretzel* would never just . . ."

There was the ghostly chill
that ruffled the house whenever
my mother aired it: it could as well
be made of cardboard then.

I cried.

At Dunbar the next day,
wedged in a huge rubber ring,
spinning beneath an azure sky,
I finger my wound

recalling how that morning
my mother had lightly brushed an eye
as my uncle drove me away.

Now, tilting my head back,
I feel I am flying; till a freak wave
licks my trailing buttocks, like fire.

Holiday down South

One afternoon, draped in cast-offs,
we performed a plotless masque
beneath the laden plum-tree.

At interval, we poured lemonade from a jug
that needed two hands. Laughing, they tipped it
beneath their deck-chairs.

They preferred the cider my uncle served
from a fat barrel by his shoulder.
They preferred their wartime stories.

Later, an aeroplane droned by the moon
and all my aunt's chintzy roses
were blotches of blood.

Rising from her nest of blankets, my sister
called my *Silly*. "One 'plane doesn't make
a war," my aunt smiled.

And so they thought to have calmed me.

"Ever seen such plums?" my uncle asked.
Those last ones were the colour of old blood:
the slightest pressure split them.

Mucking out the Byre

The men drew lots for summer's
worst job. They wore their stoutest boots.
"Are you in or out?" Then the door
was shut and only a funnel of light
came through a skylight in the roof.

The others laughed as the loser
flicked a fag-end their way, picked up
his shining grape and climbed into
the boxed-in quarter, where summer's
calves had wintered. Three infested feet

he would have to shovel away.
At first he dug his fork well in,
but the thatched muck was too heavy—
the men whistled derisively
until he had found his rythm.

When he was through the first layers,
the joking had ceased. Everyone's
grip tightened round starting handles,
spades, improvised farmyard weapons—
an alert rural riot squad.

"There's one!" The shout stabs the thick air.
My eyes track a grey blurr racing
round the broken rim of the fence,
till one man sharpens my focus
with a crushing blow from his spade.

It falls like a beanbag; its mouth
edged with blood. This first was a prize
in itself, but for the others
there could only be the manner
of their going. Accuracy

and style drew shrieks of approval.
I stayed tight against the stone wall
watching the men swivel and sweat
like automata come to life:
till the first sprawling nest of rats—

baby rats—was uncovered
in a warm, fecund catacomb.
Two of them, bald as thumbs, with blind,
bluish lumps for eyes, are skewered
on one prong and scraped off, like shit.

The King and Queen

Even on humid summer days, the King
could be seen, striding along Princes Street
in rubber boots. From red double deckers,
our bare thighs separating from our seats,

we all followed the tilt of his helmet,
the polythene breastplate bound up with string,
till only the sun held him like a shiny
black beetle. But, as if he might bring

some judgement crashing down on his tin crown,
he took no notice of our calls; nor changed
his stride for anyone—people parted
before him and, in his wake, arranged

themselves into backward-looking tableaus.
What had *reduced* him to this state? The word
when paraphrased to us, with all its dark
edge of meaning, was adult and absurd:

we saw a beachcomber gracing our streets
and wondered what luck had shot him free
to speak with the bright tongues of fiction: "Come,
all life's games of chance radiate from me."

The Queen was more twisted nomenclature
and her patch remained the brooding East End,
where she shuffled from bin to bin, searching
generous butts. She seemed broader than ten

of us—though God knows what she lived on:
always in the same old coat, her legs bare.
Sometimes, when she had pissed herself or cried
bare-faced, we would cross from the awful cares

that gaped before us. For, compared to her,
the King was a cosy retirement card—
"Gone Fishin'", "Happy Days"; but all women
that age could be our mothers, and far

deeper than the King's genteel "Reduction",
this tramp struck home. What was it to be free?
We were drawn on by sickening eddies
towards an uncharted and portless sea.

The Master of Vailima

Home no more home to me, whither must I wander?
                          (Robert Louis Stevenson)

The Master of Vailima leans on the high
    veranda. He is posterity's dandy; a rickle

of shins, shrouded in white, black-belted
    as a buccaneer. Behind him the shadows

of airy, redwood rooms and the green mount of Vaea
    rising. Here, surely, a spirit could breathe—

far from the haar and coasts bristling
    with patriarchal achievement. Illness, it was,

sealed the child in him—implacable, Blind Pew,
    like a claw around his wrist, leading him

to the darkened room, where archipelagos of leaves
    were mapped out in sunlight and Cummy's voice

rolled out, like the sea. And illness it was
    which, at last, set him free

to a more wholesome escape than piss-ups
    at Rutherford's and the *frisson*

of childhood whores. Free, he became
    the world's eye: a bright lens turning

over the dark and distant oceans, making "of his mind
    a map", where the restless traveller

need never stop. Even at Vailima—the prayers
    for his gothic tribe of dependents; kneeling

over the indifferent earth—was there ever
    an arrival? Was this desperate encampment

home? The trade winds, like an insistent
    amanuensis, script over the watery graves:

"There are other kinds of scaffolding, father:
    lives to make, as well as save."

Words

The oar creaked in its sprocket
like a rotten tooth—yet we were carried
across the Almond, from city to country
as if by magic.

Hand in hand along Dalmeny shore, I thought—
how beautiful she is, and told her so.
Laughing uneasily, she gave me
the top of her head to kiss.

I was one of a line of blessed men—
men with Continental Leanings: down the ages
the Levelling sunlight had fallen on all
our uncollared, unbuttoned, white shirts.

"I don't want to get married," I said—
conjuring the words from the faint sea breeze,
my heart beating faster with excitement
and surprise.

And again—later or earlier—alone
in Princes Street, on the clearest East coast day,
I ran my eye round the city's towers

and I said to myself, "City, lovely city,
I must leave you." And the words flew from me,
free as pigeons I never thought or cared
would come to roost.

II

The River

1. EVENING SKETCH

Night squats on the grey estate: the river,
the roads turn black. Up a deserted side-street
darkness tears away from a nakedly
lit shop-front: Mini-Cabs For Hire. Inside
a man, slumped on a frayed red settee, snores
before the T.V.'s vertiginous greens.
C & W, here is your soul: in this glimpsed
interior or on the waterfront,
where the hamburger man stares idly
through his caravan's tight lozenge of light,
as two drunks, leaning into each command,
duel over their mongrel's affections.
Later, in a bright, packed snug, one will lie
amongst broken glasses, weeping her shame,
as *he* casts narrow glances round the bar—
blue eyes blazing with fright and challenge.

2. FLIGHT

Someone kicks the blown pod of a mixer
to life, triggers a flock of birds. They rise
from their clenched roosts in a dark fan: splinters,
filings—a taut hawser, suddenly snapped,
disintegrated, sucked beyond a grey
zeppelin of cloud to where riverside
chestnuts shadow the milky amnion
and we appear—we, the giddy ones—corks
on the earth's black waters. We are learning
slowly about pain: that however deeply
we trawl it, we will bob up again
into this cool, indifferent morning.
Here, to pluck the last overblown roses;
to watch birds fall on the lawn, like ashes.

3. FLOOD

Rather the sour dampness of her own rooms
than a Home. Rather the sofa's chaos—
the urinous news, the anti-diet—
than the more orthodox regime.
Here to wait Death, like one of Cavafy's
Senators, vast camiknickers soaking
up the blasting gas fire. Only a flood
could move her and, when the waters do rise,
two policemen arrive. Her neighbours stand
at the edge of the great creeping puddle,
when, in the beam of a torch, she edges
her zimmer forward. Her hand trembles briefly
on her shawl—a gift meant for Christmas—
but her light-trapped face shakes off its tears.

4. NIGHT WALK

In the evening park, swings hang preter-
naturally still: horseshoes of packed ice
catch the pale moonlight. Deep in his enclosure,
the fallow deer tucks his nose into his haunches
till he is perfect form—stone or mask:
though the dark seaweed of his horns crowns him
like an ancient curse. Through black conifers
the creme turret of the local museum
commands the town: its death mask is a prize
amongst the rusting leg-irons. And what
has this chalk edifice to tell—the thin lips,
the fin of the nose—of evil? The moon
sidles from a cloud, looks down on the blank
physiognomy of this night, this park, this town.

5. SUMMER RITUAL

On hot days, the boys left their riverside
campfire beneath the viaduct to swim
and clown about in the centre of town.
Desperate beings! The sun ran down
their knuckled spines; dried the wet scallops
their buttocks left on the wall in lines. Soon
a challenge grew: who could walk the white seam
of the weir, cupping water in his hands?
We waved back at countless waxen soles, watched
armless bodies totter and twist, to see
who could seal their sparkling gift and bear it
across the river. In the end, one was dredged
from a feculent pool; his pale face veined
by a lime-green weed, his fingers dripping tears.

6. THE RIVER BY NIGHT

It's strange to hear that clear bell toll over
the containers' nocturnal manoeuvres:
it reminds of *pensions* in foreign towns
with the shutters open wide and, as here,
lights strung out along a river. The water
ruffles like old flesh; each eddy drawing
a meniscus of light: an infinite
tremor of energy. In such domains
I read the capacious remedies of love,
the twisted spools of memory, which burn
but don't go out. Yet this night river soothes
something deeper still, I can no more name
or touch than foretell where tomorrow's gulls
will land—or try the hunger of their beaks.

Film School

"Love?" she said. "It too's a load of crap.
At its best *modus vivendi*—its worst a trap;
a fair means or foul just to get you in the sack."
And, after this screening, she will smile sweetly as we unpack
these looming images of power and lust and embed them
in her argument. But, scarlet nails round a tall, cool stem,
do we really need a semiologist to tell us this truth:
that for her the come-on is money; for him—beauty, youth?

I see a clearer need. Late night at the Thirsty Oak,
the air rank with smoke, feet sticking to a carpet soaked
with spillage. Under a spotlight, the band sing, "Help me
make it through the night," while those seeking a key
to unlock the twirling cage of their lives, shuffle round,
looking for anyone with whom to establish common ground.
On ripped, plastic seats, others who have got it made, clutch, kiss,
sit back and anticipate, tonight at least, a kind of bliss.

Declaration

I shall live in the darkest lair,
let no one know that I am there.
I shall do this in love's name
until love comes home again.

I shall live on bones and hair
and if I choke, let no one care.
I shall do this in love's name
until love comes home again.

I shall breathe the foulest air,
never try to slip my snare—
there is nothing I won't bear
until love comes home again.

*Extensive reworking of three spells
to take on other forms by Isobel Gowdie.*

Case Studies

Dumfries Kirk Session: winter 1706

Jean Brown
stoutly maintains
she is a Turner
of Riddles, a Weaver
of Spells; that *her* spirits
killed Robert McCaw
and cured her
of her sickness.
More: that these
spirits lie
carnally with her;
are in fact
her maker.

The kirk session
does not know
what to do
with her—or
for that matter with
taciturn John McNairn
who charmed home
his favourite mare,
weak with hunger
and bitter cold:
a peeled twig,
the devil's lore.

Witches

*Sources: three photographs of collaborators
taken by Robert Capa in Chartres in August 1944;
voices from witch trials, Dumfries 1650s.*

I

Brought to the Prefecture de Police,
*she must confesse her sin and scandall
and be rebuikit* with the rest. Already the courtyard
is littered with their shaved pelts.

Capa takes them, in their shame, standing alone
against the crumbling brick wall, either side of a sturdy
wicker chair—a parody of bourgeois domesticity—
this trinity of mother, daughter and new-born child
a terrible foulness has marked.

The story goes, *He did command
that she fall down and worship him
and if she wold not worship him that she wold worship
his staff and if she wold not worship him or his staff
that she wold worship the Divell.*

But now none can tell whether Death's Head,
fear or sheer sadness moulded the passivity
in her still-young face, dulled her averted eyes
till the blind softness at the bald nape of her neck
is as eloquent about her fate. (Note though the dimple
set in her chin: the Devil indeed is dissembling.)

Her mother's dark-shadowed head is flanked by Buddha's ears,
but—in her powerful fifties—she peers at us
through severe owl-like glasses more as a teacher
whose children disappoint. Only the open mouth

betrays horror. That and the right hand which grasps
a fistful of her long black dress, holding onto temper
or dignity, while her left grips an empty feeding bottle,
a ghostly ring of milk at its bottom.

With these two hands she cradles the power
which comports her daughter, fills that vessel
with the impulse to mother. Thus, the heavy arms which fold
round the swaddled child, which support the thumb-
sucking, dark-haired head are a vague
tribute from mother to mother.

II

In carnival atmosphere, they are swept
through the cobbled streets of Chartres
under the perfect eye of the cathedral. She holds her baby
close, stares into its face for the only innocence.
The gendarme escorting them smiles like a traffic cop:
this crowd is mostly women and fearless girls
at their heels in floral summer frocks.

They callit her base jade howre and ane witch
and they laugh in her face: one young woman
addressing us with such abandoned beauty
it seems her love chimes with the camera.

And should she not laugh on a warm August day
when the flags of Liberation barely ruffle, when the fear-
mongers become the afraid? Laugh, that for this moment at least,
all evil, all the worst possible luck has landed
with another and she been called to book?

III

Now Capa leaves them to return
to their ever-changed house; to close shutters,
to live in shadows, to turn mirrors to the wall.
A million pleasures will become strangers to them—
arranging flowers, finding comedy in fault, breaking bread
                                                    with neighbours.

Instead, they will sit in silence bonded by blood and despair—
till their door is chapped
till the first stone is thrown
till they hear "German Bastard" in every idle shout.

Hair will not soothe them
nor the crying child. Between the three of them,
how can the water of love ever flow freely?

Still, the world will not weaken.
By such tiny crimes, the Great Horrors
are constituted. "God help us," cried Elizabeth Maxwell,
tried by Thomas Crauffurd, the Prodder—
"We have meslet skins, we sit neir the fyer."

Breakfast-Time

Maybe altruism is our most primitive attribute, out of reach, beyond our control. Or perhaps it is immediately at hand, waiting to be released, disguised now, in our kind of civilisation, as affection or friendship or attachment.
(Lewis Thomas)

The fallow deer throws his antlers back
and barks his lust down the barrel
of his stretched throat,
ripping the still soft belly of morning.

The doe, nipping last leaves from a high branch, stops.
Her hooves fall soundlessly on the hard earth
as gulls, like floured chaff, scatter over the town:
its volumes bland in contusions of sunlight.

If I switched on the television now,
I could watch a distant city fall—black smoke
like a pall above it; its bodies frozen in self-
sealing sacks To Be Disposed Of later.

It's a disembodied story with a murderous plot.
We're shown a different detail each day—
this blinded child, that bleeding old stump.
Deja vu aggregates of hatred.

I sit at my window, watching
blue tits squeeze a mash of peanut
through wire mesh. They rotate in pairs
from their perch on the T.V. aerial

jealously guarding their turn.
Do you know, they're the neatest things, topsy-
turvily feeding or angrily pecking glass
for an aphid on the other side.

A biologist might say I am coded
for blue tits. They release in me great waves
of warmth and affection—the message
sparking across my cerebellum is Reach Out.

Out. Out on the bare crook of the tallest tree,
the crow's beak, like an old flint, cracks.
"Kaa," it says, "Kaa." Winter closing in
on a world balanced between love and more terror.

The Ship

Once proud barques moved up the river,
bringing wine and spices from Bordeaux.
The small ports carried currencies
fat with foreign vowels: doucadouns,
Spanish *reals*, Old English groats.

There's still profit in their situation:
a fine view over the river's curve,
of a small white sail tacking upstream,
the kinetics of oyster catchers,
their beaks flaming in the sunset.

Most years though bring only more silt
and haafnetters shaking their heads at
so much silver for the whisky's gold
and the poor salmon catch. Where once
ploumdames, liquorice, the finest

French linen were sold, the Hotel
directs its Sunday drinkers as a
carpark overflow. While bored children,
fearing their clipped futures may lie
in the mysterious apathy

of the bus shelter (those silent
coupling bikes) use ragged pot-holes
as a stone-horde, a reservoir of splash.
Then one year, like a queen honouring
a lost colony, a French bulk carrier

docked. Its picture in the paper
took up two pages; a grey mass
suckling the small white-washed village.
Families drove from the nearby town
to picnic in its lee, for France

had never seemed so far away, nor all
they stood in, owned and ate, testament
to the ancient dignity of trade.
And yet from its shadows, I felt
a darker world tugging at me

with the strangest undertow; saw
caps rain down as a liner slid
into a grainy sea and banks
of lives, which had all been lived, wave
wildly from every gleaming rail.

It was like finding one's future
somewhere in the past: a fine silt
which worked its way into each crack
of all the plates which float our lives,
causing each one, in turn, to fall

like petals from the hull. Gasping,
I clung to the crude raft of work;
in darkness, cleaved to a body's
warmth; turned small-talk to rivets
before I dread the depths of sleep.

Then one night, after a few drinks,
three of us left the rooted crowd,
picked our way through the black brooding
graveyard of overnight containers—
and boarded. The insistent throb

of disco was a sounding-board
for silence—insectlike, complete—
as we felt our way to the prow
like smugglers. There we took command.
The river brought us the faint tang

of the sea and endless shots of night;
within which we lost the landscape's
bearings. Mountain, forest, hillsides—
all dissolved in darkness. Lights
sparkled here and there along the river's edge—

the friendly lights of settlements
where succour would be given to each
who had a need. So this—this
was Nile, Amazon, Limpopo . . .
Linking arms, we made a pact

to dissolve what we'd become, to hold
onto this profligate world
of dreams and possibilities,
as the dull clang of living history
sounded hard beneath our feet.

A Favourite Stretch of Disused Railway

Dalbeattie to Dumfries line

I

Turn sharp right off the forestry track.

You're on a path of large granite chips
shrouded by silver birch. This will lead you
onto the viaduct. Here the birch become
glossy saplings, the stones one long rockery
for wild strawberry, for the palest green tree shoots.

From here you can see how well-appointed
the big houses are; their stables boarded up now
and windows broken, but your eye led to them
by the fold of the landscape, by the command
of trees, as surely as in any Claude.

A hawk skims the variegated tops
of an arboretum—cyprus, copper beech,
improbable monkey puzzle. Your spirit
goes with it—for you are halfway
to flying here, riding these great arcs of air
with only a mane of rough red stone to hold onto.

II

At the end of the viaduct, a broken grey stile.
The path weeps into a green baize, stitched
with tiny white stars. A moped, clogged with rust,
stands alone; the garish flowers on its petrol tank
almost fading as you look. Playful ghosts
crowd in on you. Old beech trees
spread their arms in perfect planes.

III

When the path becomes a path again,
it is a sodden mud-track, a fine silt
of rootless earth, whose depth you could not judge,
if not aware of that broken vertebrae beneath.
One pool, clear of the choking tagliatelle of algae,
still shows the sharp edges of a few pinkish pieces
of granite. Everywhere else, marsh marigolds
sway imperiously on teased-out stems.

IV

This vegetable world delivers you
into a dark valley of blasted rock, where the ghosts
of a hundred dead wills feel exotic. The purest water
drips down a dank face to be caught on the tip
of each asterisk of moss and become—up close—
a reredos of opalescent drops. Green railings
of nettles crowd the base of this achievement:
sycamore, birch, ash stubbornly cling.

V

As I see it, passing through this gorge,
when the carriage was cast into shadow, a passenger—
one bull-necked, ruddy-complexioned, studying
the market-price of lambs—sighed dust and smoke
up spidery nostrils, laid his paper on his lap
and glanced up at the blur of rock, so that

when it was past, his blinking eyes just caught
the sun hitting the heraldic bank of wild rose
and giant daisy. And, as the perfect landscape
opened out before him, he heard the auctioneer's
breathless chanting become the sound
of a speeding train.

The Great Outdoors

Eagerly, I climbed after you to a coign
where the broom was unreal—a curdling
of the richest yolks. Beyond it, fishermen
scrambled over rough black rocks

to the sea's swollen edge. Cumuliform
stencils of sand stretched out
across the bay. Suddenly a sound,
as of silence crumbling, caused me

to glance up from the pink campion
I was cupping in my palm to catch you
poised over that part of the path
where granite snuggled into a dyke.

A white signpost read FOOTPATH one way,
FOOTPATH another, and in the bright sun,
I could not tell whether you regarded me
playfully or mockingly and I wondered

which of these arrows you would follow:
your knapsack between your shoulderblades;
the rationed butter seeping
through the tiny combs of bread.

Summer Running

The chestnut that all winter
cast broken rods on the water
now dips a head, full as a bison's,
to drink.

The once bald arterial oak
crowns the field like a green
roccoco keep.

And our quiddity? Our glory?

We arrive—new-born—
beneath the green light of birch arrows,
hoping, if we run hard enough,
to live in a season, where the tang of wild garlic
is the only hint of loss

and the haze of bluebells is everywhere,
like desire.

III

Rough Seas: Three Postcards

I

You can just make out our hotel about
to be wiped out by a mountainous wave.
A nice fiction perhaps, but in fact today
the sea is calm as glass and already
Sally is spreadeagled with the rest,
impressing the sand with her tan. Not me,
I feel more the pull of rough seas—great plumes
of spume rearing over an empty prom:
a winter image on cheap card that yet
can wolf down the summer souvenir wrack.
Once, as children, didn't we thrill to anything,
racing the gentle tide? Now we only
like the sun to touch us; though rough seas call
us to their edge, drench us with simplicity.

II

You can just make out our hotel about
to be wiped out by a mountainous wave.
Not so: just a swell and constant drizzle
keeps us all locked in a seaside cliché.
I've taken to walking alone along
the wetblack promenade, drunk on salt-air,
till, cold as a bobbing gull, I seek refuge
next to a leering postcard stand. I wrap
my stinging hands round a clear plastic cup
and stare out with all other eyes. I find
Sally's love comes at me now like a huge
toppling wave, careless of whatever I am.
At this grey edge, churlishly, I wish
for one who wanted me less, but loved the more.

III

Waves slam the promenade and explode
past the crenelated facades; as much
creature and fire as water, they hang
like a taunt over the routed sea-front.
Driven indoors, we drain each bulletin:
eight brave men needlessly *Lost at Sea*.
We are shown the beast licking round the rocks
where their craft was broken; the ragged skelfs
that must be last contact for all whose pride
the greedy lens can't touch. I read "The Wreck . . .",
let the language break over me, but all
seems rhetoric to the plain salty truth—
that for some people Rough Seas can never be
metaphorical: nor words enshrine their pain.

Sisters

A Middle European Romance

I

Before the war each in turn had loved him.

They had sat *en famille* round the oval oak table
as light from the crystal candelabra polished
the blushes on their cheeks; picked out

the devilment in his deep blue eyes. Three loves
he had taken at their greatest giving: three faces
tilted towards him like lilies

time had melted into one. But each brow,
in turn, had furrowed at the vague longing
led him on, tied his tongue, made them lack

till it seemed difficulty became his art.
Perhaps the war was some kind of calling,
so hurriedly he left the old estate;

the sullen ferryman, whose look said, "Mark,
it'll all be changed here when you get back."
And true, each headline saw him helplessly staked

to an old world that was turning from them. Faced
with their own No Man's Land, they made the best
of what was left; bar one. Her dress

billowed in the water like a sack of corn.

II

Now—out of the blue—he has returned

to interrupt their commensal couplings
with reminders of earlier passion. In cool rooms,
they wait for him, reading or fanning memory

till the bare wires of some clumsily improvised
fitment—say a car lamp to read by—will cause
waves of melancholy to wash over them.

Then the simplest of mirrors traps them
in dark corners. Only the youngest (she who reads
into his distance a form of grace)

daring to look, looks on. "Do you never long
for love?" asks his elderly aunt: all this knowledge,
yet something that spreads like a stain

over his sentient heart. "There's that chill
in the air again," his uncle says, as a swan
curls a gloved arm around itself and shines

in the moonlight. Can time, after all, outlive
wisdom? How can he reach out more? "You'll see . . .
You'll see, it'll all even up in the end.

Joy . . . sadness . . . We all have an equal share."
But *he* just stares at the black gap of the barn
and recalls a day when it was splashed with sunlight

and he counted out single grains from the frayed
corner of a sack, while someone sobbed
and he revelled in his choices.

III

At the cemetery, the youngest sees him
tearing leaves from the unmarked grave. He'd whimpered,
she tells them all later; pretended she just wasn't there.

No one mourns his leaving—this lover of earth
and of air. They are too busy stacking autumn's preserves
to wave to the creaking ferry; to ask if he'll be back.

The Leap

Wherever we walk today
spokes of light follow,
catching the silver of the dry

grey gate, the lost blue agate
in your eyes. We have been hard up
against it for months: a rot

of the will which read
any heart's sinking as truth. Now
a woodpigeon exploding upwards

can touch me with envy and shame.
Why did we surrender last summer,
when we explored the forest

like children, designating
caution and time as sin? Now
to be grateful for anything

breaking the silence;
the scattered toadstools between us
poking through the no-go grass.

From habit we arrive at the small loch,
cupped in the forest's heart.
Here the rough present shocks

a gentler past. Glumly I lob
a stick onto the calm surface
for Jet—the kamikazi black lab—

most trusting and seductive of dogs,
who launches himself like a parachute
sending water into a rage

before a head—proud and still—surfaces
making for the bank. I think now
lack of faith, and cowardice

have made cowards of us both
as Jet drops the black baton at our feet
and marks us with his radiance.

Study in Iconography

The broken bitch hirpled
half-paddled towards us
across the sawdust floor.
Colour and flesh had drained

to its overblown rump.
As if taunted by a mad
puppeteer the hind claws
pumped; yet the more it raked,

the more white lattice
was revealed, the fresher
the torment, it seemed.
How like the squat dog

we'd picked out, carved
in sunlight by the cathedral
door. It too was worn
into another life

yet, muzzling the stiffness
of time, its cracked jaws craned
to the hooded peasant
that stood on its back,

strained for revenge, to be
free from this bleak
iconography of hatred.
Now this half-living

loving dog turns to me
one grey marbled eye,
a set of bruise-blue nipples.
You hold your sandal

to a particular itch—
feed it a cone of croissant.
"You don't believe such things
deserve to exist, do you?"

you say, fancying you see
some Pantocrator that sits
in my soul, consigning
the poorer half of life

to the unforgiving,
unending jaws of night.
Such haughty righteousness
I could not fight; in fact

years later, still
I am troubled by that foot
in the small of my back,
my jaws denied their bite.

The Rondanini Pietà

We learn from a letter of Daniele de Volterra
to the nephew of the Master, Leonardo Buonarroti,
that six days before his death
he worked all day on this statue.

It is the revised version of what was begun
seven years earlier, when he was already eighty-two.
Of that, the legs of Christ and a severed right arm
remain. The slack legs, the smooth thighs begin

a gentle, upward-flowing movement ending
in the diagonal alignment of the heads of Mary,
who supports him—and Christ. As in the Pietà
in St Peter's, the pose is impossible, but there

similarity ends. Fifty years have passed.
Fifty years have taken care of his concern
for virtuosity, for rendering the softness
of a face, the fluid cascades of a dress.

And what we have instead is the image
of something that suffers and is true. Figures
that are almost shadows: hatched
with imperfection, slender, infirm;

their barely-featured faces staring
into an endless pit of sorrow. And what we have
is that throwback right arm: polished, strong;
standing by the pair of them like something

lopped from a body so the body might be free.
"I saw Michelangelo at work," writes the traveller,
Blaise de Vigenère. "He had passed his sixtieth year
and although he was not very strong

yet in a quarter of an hour he caused more splinters
to fall from a block of marble
than three young masons in three or four times
as long. No one can believe it

who has not seen it with his own eyes.
And he attacked the work with such energy
and fire that I thought it would fly into pieces."
Even accounting for increase in age then

it's a mystery why he did not hack off
that bodiless right arm and be done: but left it
almost as if he meant us to contemplate how far
he had travelled from the interests of his youth.

Catterline

for Joan Eardley

A broken bannister of cottages—a track
plunging to a bay like a scallop
whose grassy headlands today
shimmer like Seurats.

Here, in number one,
the cancer at her back—breakfast
poked through the window—to the end
her life bled into her art.

Four or five of the works they found later
stuffed into holes for the rain—
"Ah Joan," they say softly,
who knew her then: "She had nothing."

But—to her—if there was light enough,
that light was all. On the wildest days,
her easel cairned down, her canvas
took the brunt of the storm

for as long as time would allow.
So that now,
even if you see Catterline
on a day more fitting to Cap Ferat

than the grey North Sea, still
through the sunshine you can feel
dark elemental rhythms,
white breakers crashing in.

Longing

Were we there
on that basking island
the still loch at its centre
where the blue heron stood
unruffled at our dancing?

Were we there
splintering the calm water
a shoal of silver mackerel
clapping tails in unison
at such a salty kiss?

Were we there? I wonder
now I am here
where lonely peewits call:
beyond this poem,
the White Island warrior—
my shield holding my longing in.

Inishere, Aran Islands

IV

Absent Lover

Each morning I lie awake,
conjuring your body beside me;
laying my head on the still brown
small of your back, kissing
a pale, warm buttock.
                              But at night
we leave the strictures
of time and place to float off,
like Chagal's couple over the still town;
like Kokoschka's to love in the midst
of a passionate universe.

In Central Park

Each weekend they come to dance
beneath their equestrian king
to the music of a large cassette.

In circles and horseshoes, their hands
resting on shoulders, their feet
kicking to left and to right

then—hey presto—a procession
taking two steps forward, one back:
come together and twirl and forward and back.

A patterned language, once learnt,
should stick, yet each week they are drawn
to the concrete dial surrounded

by a thousand other pursuits
to come together and twirl and forward and back—
an insistent tick saying:

this is what we were, what we are,
what we want to be. An easy-
seeming language, yet we did not join in;

still trusting to a necessary silence,
wary of the hidden intricacies
of movement which have wrong-

footed us before. Standing with you
on the fringes of that crowd, nodding
a smiling refusal beneath autumn trees

seems an Indian Summer now.
Now the time of assimilation has passed,
how clumsy words can be

as we move them around—forward and
back, forward and back—reminding ourselves,
in weakness, of the beauty and the ease

of the dance.

Going Downtown

As the train pulls away
from 72nd. Street,
a man in his thirties, swaying
slightly on plimsoled feet,

comes in from another carriage.
(Institutionally) at ease, he takes up
a position by the door, centre-stage,
a crushed paper cup

in one hand. With the other,
he grips the gleaming metal rail;
his eyes fixed over
our heads on the blurred subway wall.

Then, when confident of the motion,
he runs a free hand
through his long blond quiff. As if at some Station
of the Cross, his fine head

tips back and in a monotone
he speaks . . .
"Could I have your attention
for a minute, ladies and gentlemen, please?

"I'm not, nor do I ever wish to be
a panhandler. I don't enjoy
doing this, as I hope you can see
but I have no choice.

"I was released from prison
last week with nothing—no job,
no place to stay, no money. I've learned
my lesson and I don't wanna rob

"no more. As I said before:
I don't intend to be doing this for long;
but for the moment I gotta live.
So please . . . Give."

And he moves round the skimpy
congregation, proffering his cup.
He walks with a slight limp:
his thankyous reverential, never looking up.

I see him at the next station
between carriages,
pausing for a moment's meditation
or rage

before he takes a deep breath
and with shoulders drawn back
carries himself
across that black-gathering gap.

A Taxi of My Choice

We are riding up Riverside
in a yellow taxi of my choice;
a beast so powerful, we roll
together and part as it hits
each wave of traffic. The noise
of the suspension at each jolt

so harsh, we feign wide-eyed fear,
yet your commentary runs on . . .
When I see a drunken man push
another to the wall and clear
in the streetlight they kiss, then
disappear into the shadows,

you tell me "Cruising" was shot here—
an area of black warehouse walls
and discrete neon signs. And black
too is the Hudson as it sheers
away from light, seeming to fall
into silence like a soft ballad.

And speaking of which, over there
is Hoboken, where ol' Blue Eyes
came from: finest fixer of place
for those who must move on. I share
his feel for this city, the rise
of the wall of lit, shattered glass

to our right—each splinter a life.
An hour ago, above it all—
"The closest some of us will get
to heaven," the brochure says—love
took a back seat, as we ogled
what creativity and greed

could do. "That bar of light is Fifth.
That's Brooklyn"—piecing together
the city for me, like some vast
incandescent jig-saw; a gift
to the soul no less than St. Peter's
or Chartres. So that now, when I cast

around for some kind of statement
of what *we* collaboratively
can do, I think of that county
of light and hear your accent:
"Down from the blurr of New Jersey,
see the Statue of Liberty."

Riverside. Hoboken. Brooklyn.
Each name is a memory
within which our love can hide.
Like glitter, I have scattered them
from high. There is a part of me
in each yellow taxi you ride.

The Bathers

A gash of red:
a Yankee flag leaning from an alien crust of snow,
draws us down the beach, where
four members of the

Polar Bear Club
stand on the edge of the grey sea by a dragon's tail
of rock. They exercise
half-heartedly

against the bitter cold,
swinging arms and legs: an illiterate semaphore.
One couple—he sporting
a yachtsman's cap,

she with stetson
set jauntily on lank blond hair—does a stiff handheld
jive and, as they move, angry-
looking flesh

rubs; the full mouth
of a navel twists in an idiot's grin. Small groups
of onlookers hover
around. *They* wear

hats like trappers,
keep their cameras poised, as the Bears feather
the dying tide; evade the Million
Dollar Question:

is anyone
going under again? Watching them, such sadness
washes over me, I feel weightless
when we leave—

a high joy of the mind,
as if, at one and the same time, I were one
of those fairground structures—
a wheel or dipper,

ribs spread across
the nacreous sky—but also riding it! And you whoop
to the breeze as if on
the tremulous

cusp of that ride.
Never have I felt more free. What then, in your absence,
keeps drawing me back to that
unseasonal

landscape, those weird
creatures (my flesh now raw as theirs)? Was it the flag
below the boardwalk, I wonder,
first led me

down the white shore
or was I too born on the careless tide, like the broken
rope of shells that I scrunch
beneath my feet?

Coney Island

Love at the (Bronx) Zoo

We walk the icy paths
past frozen ponds, snowed-in enclosures,
where reeds like drifting porcupine
and black huts are all that show.

In the dim warmth of an animal house,
we linger by a tank
with a sandy-coloured,
soft-shelled turtle, the size
of my spread hand. From the long spoon
of its head, nostrils stick out
like tiny binoculars. Eyes,
two silvery stains. When it rises
from the dark green weed, its fins,
like sycamore seeds, brush the window
we peer through. So close is it
and so angled, we see

the thin loop of its down-turned mouth;
almost fancy it would speak . . .

Back in the Bronx, we don't know
which blind-eyed alley to turn down;
eventually are wrong anyway. We ride around—
a fly caught in deadly nightshade—trying
to reclaim the rim of the highway

past burned-out buildings, waste-ground;
a brazier licking the chill
off some winos.

A battered blue cadillac jerks
to a stop in front of us. Rusted panels
shake; red tail lights glare
from corroded fins. We sit tight
as the black man's black curses plume
into the winter air. We turn to each other—
sudden neophytes, who might—sleepless, speechless,
in the dark cage of night—hold their soft bodies
close; fear
for love's survival.

The Cabin

for Jill and Dick

As we shake on the rough track down avenues of birch,
I breathe your almost-there excitement—the joys
of sharing and showing. Craning forward in your seat,
you seem to leap each timid moment; as if the scene
could suddenly seep away and all beauty, all richness
be lost to the earth's dry core. Already, my mind is alive
with Indians, with the nervous calm of deer drinking.

We pull up on a seed-strewn clearing and I follow you—
Leatherstocking in hanging jeans—to the edge of a clear coin
of water and at last we're there—the Frisch Cabin at Lost Lake.

Two boats have wintered here; in the silence, by the old stove,
by the random harvest of books and holiday flotsam. They yield
two canvas chairs, you set on the porch—or is it the prow?—
and straight away we unwrap great wedges of turkey and salami
with salad and a six-pack—all for a fraction of city prices!
Sure, this time of day it's warmer elsewhere. The spring sun
is on that stub of a rose you planted last year and light
dances on the ribs of the beached blue boat by the jetty.
But twenty-five years have shaped this habit, this life.

"This place was the death of ambition. Three hundred dollars
and I had what they were all striving for." Such as the sight
of fourteen whoopers. We watch their watery rushes
                                             at each other,
how they sit squat as tugboats in their anger, tucking
their necks back, so you can almost see the sour beaks pinch.

One day these fourteen will be two. A flight of Canadian geese
pass overhead. Tilting back, we let their angelwings carry us
through the spare silver lattice of birch and ash. I pull my head—
woozy with lunchtime beer—back on a long, loose, goose neck.

"When Jill and I were first married, we'd sit each evening
on either side of the fire and read. Have a beer. Not talking.
Another beer. Then, when we'd get up, I'd be out of it, lying
on that bed, watching the moonlit waters tremble
on the ceiling, drunk as a . . ."

Skunk cabbage grows in the forest's dank creases.
It doesn't stink to me, nor spear-shaped and elegant
is it anything like cabbage. Lime-green, each leaf seems the tip
of something broken out the minute before you see it.

"When I die, I want to be buried beneath a tree next to that lake—
though the way things are going, they'll chop it down
                                                    the next day."
Then what better than skunk cabbage to mark the spot?
                                                    Or that rose?

The Storm

In the humid late afternoon
I twin your bed-spread body
with the phone, lying snug
in its dead-dog cradle.

How many *Elegies for Marilyn*
are composed this way? The mute
cityscape beyond, the squat
rockets of its water-towers

so many primitive monuments
to the capriciousness
of fecundity and desire:
while further still the silver

loom of a bridge offers
fragile promise of release . . .
Like a somnambulent swimmer's,
your legs twitch again:

how I wish, with you,
my body could float free
from this world of unsatisfactory
surfaces—this stifling womb

where somewhere
above you, another's blood
is pounding you down—and find
some disinterested blue element.

. . .

In the next room, we hear
the gathering storm flick
randomly through the pages
of an open book, till finally

maddened by some secret
the print will not yield,
it rifles backwards and forwards,
rumbling and spitting disgust.

Naked, we crouch
by the window, watching the rain,
shaken to be caught between apartments,
twist, turn, cast skin on silver skin.

It's then we notice the ailanthus tree
that grows in the crotch of two
apartment blocks, normally
placid as a pot-plant. Not now.

Now, as if lightning had triggered
something at its heart, its shy
carapace has cracked and each spread palm
shakes in a vortex of desire

as stars of etiolated lip-
shaped leaves share their secret
softness with the lightning's quick eye.
But no matter the thrashing power

of this wild Creature of the Deep—
this fulcrum, this victim of the storm—
the concrete thighs against which it beats,
contain it, their feet held by the lowering sky.

· · ·

When it's all over, we walk out
into a glistening, metallic street,
where every iron belly carries
transparent teats, begging

to be shaken. The air itself
has a new fragrance—a translucent
presence. Fresh, green, it seems
strangely enriched by the same source

that so recently was redolent
of the hothouse—mossy, jungly, dank,
tangling our every thought, our best
intentions in that darkened room.

Need

In the shallow water
of the weir, gulls
watch for their supper.
Ungainly they flop
first one way,
then another, as if
an invisible hand
shakes them
the way they
will a fish. I'm
floundering too
without you—not
knowing which
fishing pools
to try or how
to read the current.
I need to be air-
borne again; like a flock
of sparrows letting
the sun play
on its scattered flight.
I need to be
the swan again;
its long neck
leading it home
to its perfect element.

The Feast

Fresh Maine lobster
was laid before us—a knuckly scarlet
bouquet; the garlic butter put beside
in a dainty white cruet.

We had been told
how to proceed: first tugging the oblong head
from the fan-tail (a cosy ritual—
the breaking of bread)

before we cracked the brittle armour apart.
Now we could pick at the pink spread flesh,
dipping each flake in the butter
till we reached the grey mess

of brain. At first we glanced
at each other, checking our lobster etiquette,
but as we warmed to the task,
our appetites set

their own rules. We cracked off legs,
ripped ligaments, sucked slow on salty, hairy limbs
in our own ways; till—best of all—the claws.
It was almost whim

that I looked up then
and broke the absorption of your eye
as you lovingly kissed a morsel of that sweetest flesh
goodbye.

I pointed to a golden trickle
of butter running down your chin.
We dabbed our lips and smiled guiltily as if
it had almost been a sin

to lose each other
in this precious shared feast.
Then, leaning back, we let the waiter in
to pour out our last beer like an apronned priest.

Barges

I

The riverside air bears the sweetness
            of the first fallen blossoms;
magnolias bloom like supplicant hands.

II

Two thoughts take wing across the Hudson—
wings like a swan's that could break you.

III

We count 1 2 3 4 5 6 7 8 9 10 barges
and to each barge, another is lashed.

IV

My arm around you on the rusted railing,
we let them go like ten deep, black breaths.

Cagney Cuckolded in "The Roaring Twenties"

"What are you trying to prove, Eddie?" says Lloyd,
shaken but defiant. He has been down once already
and now stands limp in the other man's hands.
Eddie's face is a clenched fist, tightening.
He is ready to dump him again when something
remarkable happens. Beneath both their earnest,
even gaze, the bent crow bar of his brows gives
and the shadow of pain lightens with knowledge.
I gave her everything, he is thinking: the diamonds,
the singing career, the crackling crystal set—
everything and yet it is over. I should have listened:
dames like her and guys like me: champagne, hootch.
"Nothing, kid," he answers softly, dusting Lloyd's
collar down once. "I'm sorry." And he winks at her,
and with that tripping gait that says, "Don't worry,
I can handle it," he heads back to the bar,
to Panama, a real pal, who will hold and cherish
what he will now forever regard as cheap.

American Primitive

I

Like northern churches that strip faith
down to the quick, their house did with living:
as if a child had streamlined all their needs
and in the middle of the forest built this.

One small room was kitchen, parlour—berth
for the best bed. Two leaded windows kept it
light but snug; in the cavernous fireplace
both squat chest and cradle could fit.

The massive black beam support, the off-shoot ribs
which held the ceiling, spoke of an older world;
yet such solidity—the room's simplicity—
urged them on new voyages.

II

They sailed to the top of blue mountains
on paths bordered by juniper and rock—
covered by Rorschach green fungus, edged
with the blood beads of berries.

While below, in rolling sfumato,
beasts of the forest tracked down the clawless,
the soft; and vast trout thrashed through jet-black lakes
where sunset turned like a knife.

The landscape was a dark-ochre dust then;
her body light as dead leaves in flight.
The clean lines of the bed became an anchor
as he fought to gather her in.

III

In the end, a giant grizzly took her from him—
its tell-tale tufts sprouted from the patchwork quilt.
And a wilderness grew where she had stood; her poor face
blenching at the door-sized torso, even before
it leant in its bullish head.

He's worn the grizzly's back bare; he's frozen
the lust in its arrowhead teeth. But at night,
when the last dust has settled, still she cries:
"When will these chores be done . . . be done?"—
in the forest's many tongues.

Natural History

I

That scorching summer, while you worked,
I haunted the Natural History Museum, staring down
from a balcony of mandrill, koodoo and klipspringer
onto a herd of elephants mounted on an oval dais.

Across a landscape of familial shadows—
broad, proud foreheads, the slack helplessness
of haunches empty of power—two giant bulls
trumpeted mutely in the gloom.

I had a dream that each midnight, in this deep
pocket of silence, they were heard and a rich sap
spread through their bodies' thick bark.
Their trunks were first to thaw—

tired arms swinging back into circulation—
then ears like ragged kites beat the still air,
till, with imperceptible slowness, their barrel-
bodies swayed, bumped and jostled

as they climbed down—neat on their feet
as circus animals—onto the polished marble floor.
Their lily-pad footsteps echoed
in the great hall long after

they had left the nocturnal bongo
hiding in bamboo, the solitary okapi of the Congo
at ease in its cross-section of home.
And as they roamed past the ghostly light

each moribund culture, each threatened habitat
gave out, they sensed the grasslands of Central Park;
the dirt-tracks cool in the humid night—
living roots and the welcome of water.

II

Meanwhile, in your obsolescent white freezer
with its sticky door, four tea-bags float in darkness.
Screwed down in a litre glass jar, like drowned mice,
their labelled tails trail down the damp neck.

Each bleeds its own tangy spores, billowing
down like smoke, till the clear water grows brackish
and the flavour full of a slight bitterness
I can never quite get used to.

Below this totem—as I see it—plebeian,
uncomplicated, my six-pack (one down) gathers
its silver moisture. This sodden Scottish summer,
I still feel that first coldness—

each precious bead!—burn my fingertips, still hear
the early evening chink of your ice-cubes,
the says-it-all *zitz* of my Bud.
I stare from the Crags down

into the bowl of Holyrood and am hit by the sour,
damp waft of the brewery (an animal smell like must
from a mass of thick-haired follicles). I see you
arriving home tonight, putting on the fans,

cupping the sluggish air in your bottom lip
and blowing. Across the white line of cockroach-
killing boracic acid, you tug that adhesive door.
As the light hums on and the cold hits your face

and you reach for that tall dark jar, perhaps—
past your tanned and trembling arm—an eye just catches
the opaque plastic hoop of a solitary, dislodged Bud
and you sense, withdrawing from it, the ghostly

after-image of a hand. Now, now do you feel
my elephants—free at last—pass behind you,
casting their great chill shadows
of longing and of loss?

Gospel

In Canaan Baptist Church—
cavernous as a forties cinema—
an usherette in red uniform and white gloves
handed us a programme for the Easter bonanza
with the widest of welcoming smiles.

We stood at the back of the crowded balcony—
the only white faces in sight—
and when the massed choir rose in scarlet robes,
gave ourselves to their glorious voices
    Jesus walked in de wadder
    Jesus walked in de wadder
squeezing damp hands at each
tingling *coloratura*.

Thus, we swayed with the shape of their culture:
we imagined their truth—just then—
to be ours.

Remember how very good that felt.

Later, we tried to explain
that overwhelming feeling to Dick,
beatific smiles on our faces.

"Yes, only it's not true."

What suckers we were for the great
white horses of emotion, riding them
from our unlikely meeting on—
though whose truth we were plugged into then,
I still don't know.

As easy to believe the universe
has always existed as to believe
something made it.

As easy to believe we never really
loved each other as that
we ever did.

The Years

Sometimes to get their own back
our years forget us. They uncouple
and trundle off, one by one,
down gentle gradients into sidings
overgrown by giant hogweed,
there to become their own
secret memorials.

Strange creatures take up residence
in the dusty old carriages—
shiny black beetles, tenacious fungus, a dwarf.
In faded photographs, seaside towns shift
mysteriously abroad.

Still—if you're lucky—rendezvous
can take place. Behind the mighty
blind engines of passion
may come tenderness—the freight
of the years.

Still Life

Jet-lagged, ragged, I am woken by fire,
flickering in a corner of a strange room,
to find dislocated Time's made a liar
of me: the video's digital blooms
in the darkness—a cold blue insistence.
Strange to think how early I woke those mornings
to stare at your back with hot persistence—
reading your slightest sigh as a warning
I wasn't yet to invade your time-scale.
Now, locked in this lonely bubble, I listen
to autumn rain falling like friendly mail
from home and leaf through paper which glistens
with an ivory light, growing more pale
as the hours pass and a black branch thickens.

Newhaven, Connecticut